LOOKING AFTER YOUR PET

Dog

Text by Clare Hibbert
Photography by Robert and Justine Pickett

HODDER
Wayland

an imprint of Hodder Children's Books

Titles in the LOOKING AFTER YOUR PET series:

• Cat • Dog • Hamster • Rabbit
• Guinea Pig • Fish

© 2004 White-Thomson Publishing Ltd

Produced by White-Thomson Publishing Ltd
2/3 St Andrew's Place, Lewes, BN7 1UP

Editor: Elaine Fuoco-Lang
Inside design: Leishman Design
Cover design: Hodder Wayland
Photographs: Robert Pickett
Proofreader: Alison Cooper

Published in Great Britain in 2004 by Hodder
Wayland, an imprint of Hodder Children's Books.

Hodder Children's Books
An imprint of Hodder Headline Limited
338 Euston Road, London, NW1 3BH

British Library Cataloguing in Publication Data
Hibbert, Clare
    Dog. - (Looking after your pet)
    1.Dogs - Juvenile literature
    I.Title
    636.7'083

ISBN 0 7502 4299 X

Acknowledgements
The publishers would like to thank the following
for their assistance with this book:
The PDSA (Reg. Charity 283483) for their help
and assistance with the series.

Rosie Pilbeam for Border Collie dogs, Jill
Matthews of The Veterinary Hospital, Margate,
Kent; The Lord Whisky Sanctuary Fund (Reg.
Charity 283483) and Mrs Margaret Todd, MBE.

Alan Brooker (and Sam) for the picture at the
top of page 27.

Cover image: Digital Vision/Getty Images

Printed in China

Contents

Choosing a dog

The first question to ask yourself is "Why do I want a dog?"

Dogs make great companions, but they also need plenty of attention. Be sure there will be someone at home most of the time to keep your pet company or it will get lonely.

▲ This dog is cared for at a rescue centre but it wants a real home. If you adopt a rescue centre dog, ask staff to help you pick one that will fit in with your family.

▲ This puppy is a pedigree Collie. Both its parents were Collies. Puppies whose parents were different types of dog are called mongrels. They make excellent pets, too.

Most dogs need walking at least twice a day. Larger, active dogs may need long walks. Your dog will want to play out in the garden, and you will have to clean up after it. You'll have to work hard to train your dog, so it won't bite or misbehave. Dogs can also cost a lot of money in food and vet care.

Top Tips

When choosing a puppy, look for:

🐾 Clean, fluffy fur with no bare patches or sores on the skin.

🐾 A plump body, but not a fat belly (this could mean the puppy has worms).

🐾 Bright, clean eyes and ears and a damp, cool nose.

🐾 A clean bottom.

🐾 Playfulness!

🐾 No black specks which could mean the puppy has fleas.

◄ Your new puppy should look healthy and alert – just like this one!

A home for your dog

Dogs need warmth and shelter, food and water, play and exercise.

In the wild, dogs live in packs. Pet dogs are happiest being part of your pack – living in the house with you and your family. But sometimes your dog will want to be on its own and rest.

▲ Your dog will love to play with you. Buy toys that are too big for your pet to swallow and that are sturdy and well-made.

Checklist: dog kit

- Food
- Dog bed

You should provide your dog with its own bed in a quiet, cosy corner. Plastic beds are easiest to clean. Line the bed with newspaper, then add a blanket and cushion. To cut down the risk of fleas and skin problems machine-wash the cushion cover regularly and shake out the blanket every day.

▶ This dog has a clean, soft bed in a quiet place. It can rest here whenever it feels tired.

• Lead and collar with identity tag

• Food and water bowl

• Toys and chew

• Grooming brush and toothbrush

Puppy care

Puppies are adorable, but they also take a lot of looking after.

Give your puppy lots of attention and take time to play lots of games – 'fetch' is a favourite! Say your puppy's name often. Soon your puppy will know the sound and come when you call.

▶ Do you have younger brothers or sisters? You'll need to teach them to be gentle and kind to your puppy!

Training is very important. Begin training your puppy once it is fully vaccinated. See if you can find a puppy-training class in your area where you will learn how to command properly, and your puppy will learn to obey. The first lessons are house training, walking on a lead and knowing the words "Sit!", "Stay!" and "Come!".

◀ Train your puppy to obey your commands. It must learn to "Sit!" when you say so.

Top Tips

How should I train my dog?

🐾 Practise the commands with your dog for about ten minutes every day.

🐾 Be kind and patient. Don't shout at your dog and never hit it. If your pet is frightened, it will panic and be unable to understand your commands.

🐾 Praise your dog when it gets things right and, at first, reward it with a non-sugary treat.

Walkies!

Find out how
many walks your
dog will need.

▲ Going for a walk is great fun. It keeps you and
your dog fit and healthy and it is also a good
chance to spend time with your family.

The best way to get this right is to ask your vet.
He or she will know how much exercise is right
for your pet's size and age. Don't walk your dog
straight after its meal as it can get indigestion.

▼ Carry a pooper scooper and plastic bags
so you can clear up after your dog. Most
parks provide special bins for dog mess.

Pet Talk

Will my dog need a muzzle?

Some types of dog make loyal guard dogs, but they can also be dangerous – to strangers or even their owners. These dogs are not ideal family pets unless they are trained with great care. Dogs that might attack should wear a muzzle so they cannot bite anyone.

Keep your dog on the lead when you are walking near roads and be sure you can control it. The best way for you to learn how to walk your dog on a lead is to attend obedience or puppy training classes.

Remember that in some places it is against the law for your dog to be off the lead. If in doubt, keep your dog on a lead.

► Always keep your dog on a short lead if you are walking near a road. Smaller dogs may need only one or two short walks a day, while larger breeds need two to three hours of walking every day!

11

Feeding your dog

Be careful not to overfeed your dog.

Hungry dogs really do wolf down their food! A grown-up dog needs two meals a day. Try to feed your dog at the same time – early morning and early evening is best. The size of meal depends on your dog's size. Ask your vet for advice.

▼ Your dog should eat its dinner in one go. If there is food left over, you may be giving it too much.

Dogs are carnivores or meat-eaters. Feed your dog a mix of dog biscuits and tinned food. You can also give it fresh, cooked meat sometimes.

▶ Buy your dog a chew from the pet shop. Like a real bone, it helps to clean your pet's teeth and gums.

◀ You can clean your pet's teeth with doggy toothpaste. Ask your vet to show you how.

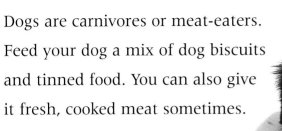

Top Tips
A healthy diet

🐾 Make sure your dog always has a supply of clean, fresh water.

🐾 Puppies need three to four small meals a day. Reduce this gradually to two meals at nine months.

🐾 Older dogs need less food – switch to a low-calorie type.

🐾 It's not kind to overfeed your dog. Being fat causes heart and joint problems, just as it does in humans.

Grooming

Keep your dog's fur in tip-top condition.

If your dog has a long coat, you will need to comb and brush it every day. Dogs with short coats can be groomed once a week. Choose a brush or comb suited to your dog's type of fur – ask your vet about this.

▶ Unless your dog has very short hair, it will need to be groomed every day. Brush gently in the direction of the fur and smooth out any tangles.

Wet walks in the country can leave your dog's fur muddy and matted. You can clean off most dirt by rubbing down with a chamois leather. But if your dog is really dirty, it will need a bath. Use bath products made for dogs and rub your dog dry with its own towel afterwards.

◀ Your dog will need its own towel. Use it to give your pet a good rub down after a walk in the rain.

▼ Short hair like this is easy to keep clean. Use a rubber grooming brush to make short coats gleam.

Top Tips
Shining coats

🐾 A wide-toothed metal comb is best for getting out tangles, but be gentle.

🐾 Use a bristle brush for general grooming.

🐾 On short-haired dogs, go over the coat after grooming with a rubber grooming brush – it'll make it shine!

Dog talk

Your dog lets you know how it's feeling in so many ways.

Watch that tail! A fast wagging tail is a sure sign that your dog is pleased to see you. A tail between the legs means your pet knows it has done something wrong and feels sad.

◀ Rolling around is playful, puppyish behaviour. It means that your dog would like you to tickle its tummy.

Top Tips

Meeting a new dog

🐾 Never ever go up to a strange dog without asking the owner first.

🐾 Crouch low, so you don't seem tall and scary.

🐾 Keep your distance, but stretch out the back of your hand slowly.

🐾 If it wants to, the dog will come and sniff your hand to check you out!

Dogs also communicate with the noises they make. A bark can mean excitement or aggression – but a well-trained dog won't bark at the wrong time. A low growl is a sign to back off. If you've just told off your dog, expect to hear a whimper – this is a bit like your dog crying.

▲ Tails talk! Dogs wag their tails when they feel friendly and happy.

► When two dogs meet, they like to sniff each other. It's their way of saying "hello!"

17

Being responsible

Have you ever seen a notice about a lost dog?

It is rare for a dog to go missing, but you should be prepared just in case. Once it starts going out, your dog must wear a collar with a tag that says your name and address. Choose a collar that fits your dog and that won't rub at its neck.

◀ Your dog needs to wear a collar and identity tag.

Ask your vet about having your dog microchipped. This is law in some countries, and a good idea wherever you are. The vet puts a tiny chip under your dog's skin that contains information about how to contact you. The chip can be read by a scanner that dog wardens and vets use.

◄ Being chipped is quick and painless. The chip usually goes under the skin at the back of the neck, where it is easy to scan.

Pet Talk

How can I make my garden safe?

If your dog sees something fun to chase, it might try to escape. Walls, fences and hedges keep dogs in. If you spot any gaps, fill them with chicken wire. Check for other dangers too, such as poisonous plants. You might want to cover the pond, especially if your pet is still a puppy.

► This dog can play safely in the garden. There is a tall fence all around it, so that the dog cannot escape.

Your healthy dog

It is your job to notice if your dog is ever ill.

► Your dog should be perky and playful. If you are worried about your pet, take it to the vet at once.

Look for the signs that your dog is healthy – it should have bright eyes, clean ears and a moist, cool nose. If you think your dog is ill, take it to the vet. Coughing or tiredness can be signs of illness. A dog that is off its food or drinking more water than usual should be checked out, too.

The vet also needs to give your pet special jabs that prevent serious diseases. The first jabs are given when your puppy is about eight weeks old. Don't take your puppy outside until it has had all its jabs and your vet says it is safe to do so. Otherwise it might catch other diseases from another dog.

◄ Vets usually inject dogs on the back of the neck. This puppy is having its last jabs. After these, it will be able to go for proper walks outside.

▶ After a walk, check your pet's paws. Sometimes, dogs get seeds or thorns stuck in their pads or next to their claws.

Pet Talk
Can I cut my dog's claws?

Check your dog's claws, especially its dew claws. These are fifth claws that your dog may have, a little way up the leg. If your dog's claws are ragged or need cutting, don't be tempted to cut them yourself. This is a job for your vet.

A trip to the vet

Your dog
should visit
the vet at
least once
a year.

Take your dog to the vet for a
yearly check-up. At the same
time, your vet will give it any
booster jabs it needs. You may
also have to take your pet
to the vet if it is ill or injured.
Always keep your dog on a lead
or, if it is a small dog, use
a carrying cage.

◀ Keep your pet on its lead when you
are in the waiting room at the vet's.
Make sure your dog sits quietly
and does not frighten any of the
other animals.

Sometimes, dogs are too ill or hurt to be cured. If this happens, your vet will suggest that your dog is put to sleep. This is very sad, but try to be brave. Your vet knows what is best and kindest for your dog.

▶ It is not easy giving medicine to a dog. You might want to ask an adult to help you.

Top Tips
Medicine for dogs

🐾 Give the correct dose – and only to the pet named on the label.

🐾 Never give human medicine to your dog.

🐾 With tablets, hold the jaws open, place far back on the tongue, then close the mouth. Stroke your dog's throat till it swallows.

🐾 With eye drops, hold the head back until the eye is totally covered with the liquid.

🐾 With ear drops, rub behind the ear so the drops trickle down deep.

Puppies – a good idea?

▲ Puppies are cute, but they can be demanding. And, after all the hard work, you will have to give them up when they go to their new families.

Don't add to the numbers of unwanted puppies.

It's best to have your dog neutered. This is an operation that the vet carries out. A female dog that has been neutered cannot get pregnant, and it helps to prevent getting serious diseases in later life. A male dog that has been neutered won't wander off after females – so it will be less likely to get lost.

Having puppies sounds fun, but it is a lot of work. The puppies will have to stay with their mother until they are at least eight weeks old. Caring for them takes up a lot of time, and it is expensive too. You will also need to find homes for them all.

▼ This mother is suckling her puppies. Pups must stay with their mother until they have stopped suckling and are eating solid food. This is called weaning.

◄ A male dog cannot get pregnant, but neutering is still a good idea. It can make the dog calmer, and more friendly.

Pet Talk

Having puppies

You might decide you want your dog to have puppies, or your dog might become pregnant accidentally. If your dog is pregnant, take it to the vet to check on its health. Ask the vet's advice about looking after it and the puppies.

Holiday time

Going on holiday is exciting, but don't forget your dog!

Your dog will be happiest with you, but that is not always possible. Not all guest houses and holiday cottages allow dogs. If you are going abroad, you might be able to take your dog with you. Check with your travel company. Remember to take proof of which jabs your dog has had.

▼ If you can, take your dog on holiday with you. If you are travelling by car, buy your pet a dog safety seatbelt.

Don't be tempted to leave your dog and just ask a neighbour to look in on it. Your dog will be lonely. Ask if it could stay with a friend while you are away – but if they have dogs too, check the animals get on first.

Taking your dog to boarding kennels may be the best bet. Visit beforehand to check that the dogs are well cared for.

◀ If you are leaving your dog with a friend, write them a checklist of what to do. Say when you normally walk your pet, and when you let it out in the garden.

Checklist: choosing boarding kennels

• Is the place clean?

• Will your dog have its own cabin?

• Is there a cosy sleeping area?

• Is there space to run and are the dogs walked at least once a day?

• Did the kennels ask to see proof that your dog has had its jabs? If not, don't go there!

▲ This dog has been left at boarding kennels. Although it will miss its owners, at least it will be well looked after.

Dog facts

Bet you didn't know that ancient Romans had 'beware-of-the-dog' signs to scare off burglars! Read on for more fun facts.

- Dogs can live for between 12 and 18 years.

- Wolves were the first guard dogs – about 12,000 years ago.

- The fastest dog is the greyhound. It can sprint at over 70 kilometres an hour.

- The ancient Greeks believed that a three headed dog, Cerberus, guarded the underworld.

- The tallest breeds of dog are the Irish Wolfhound and Great Dane. One record-breaking Great Dane, called Shamgret Danzas, stood over a metre tall at the shoulder.

- The largest dog breeds are the St Bernard and the English Mastiff. They usually weigh about 80 kg. However, the biggest Mastiff on record weighed nearly twice as much (155 kg).

- There is a star called the dog star – and it's the brightest star in the night sky.

- The first animal in space was a dog called Laika. It went into space in November 1957.

- There are over 200 million pet dogs in the world today.

- Sniffer dogs help rescue workers and police. The German Shepherd is the most common police dog – and it has about 45 times more scent-detectors in its nose than you have!

- In the Middle Ages, knights used war dogs – fierce attacking dogs that wore armour.

- Here's a story about how dogs got their wet noses – Noah's dog was said to have plugged a leak in the Ark with his nose!

Glossary

Aggression
Violent behaviour.

Boarding kennels
Places where dogs can stay and be looked after while their owners are on holiday.

Breed
A particular type of dog, such as a German Shepherd or a Border Collie.

Carnivore
A meat-eater.

Chamois leather
Soft leather, often used for polishing windows, which is also good for making your dog's coat shine.

Companion
A friend.

Dew claw
Fifth claw a little way up the inside of a dog's leg. Not all dogs have dew claws, but they are more usually found on front legs than back ones.

Fleas
Insect pests that live on dogs. Ask your vet for advice on how to get rid of fleas. You will need to treat your home to get rid of any flea eggs, too.

Grooming
Cleaning a dog's fur. This is partly done by the dog with its tongue, and partly done by you with a brush.

Identity tag
A metal or plastic disc that fixes to your dog's collar. It should be engraved with your name and address or phone number, so you can be contacted by anyone who finds your dog.

Jabs
Injections that can protect against some serious diseases.

Microchip
A tiny computer chip, the size of a grain of rice. This is placed under the skin of your dog and contains information about you, the owner. This can be read by special scanners if your dog is ever lost.

Mongrel
An ordinary dog that does not belong to a particular breed.

Muzzle
(1) The front part of your dog's face – its jaws and nose.
(2) Leather straps or a kind of cage placed over the front part of your dog's face, to stop it biting.

Neutering
Removing a dog's sex organs. This stops females from getting pregnant and makes males less likely to be violent or wander off.

Pedigree
A type of dog where both parents are from the same breed.

Pooper scooper
A plastic scoop for picking up dog mess.

Rescue centre
A place that looks after lost or abandoned animals.

Vet
An animal doctor.

Weaning
Moving a puppy on to solid foods, away from mother's milk.

Worms
Pests that live inside your dog. Your vet can give your dog worming tablets to get rid of them.

Further information

Books

How to Talk to Your Dog by Jean Craighead George
(HarperCollins Children's Books, 2000)

My Pet: Puppy by Honor Head, photographs by Jane Burton
(Belitha Press, 2002)

Dogs by Michaela Miller
(RSPCA/Heinemann Library, 1997)

Dogs by Marjorie Newman
(Oxford University Press, 2000)

The Best-Ever Book of Dogs by Amanda O'Neill
(Kingfisher Books, 1998)

Puppy to Dog by Jillian Powell
(Hodder Wayland, 2001)

Your Puppy, Your Dog: A Kid's Guide to Raising a Happy, Healthy Dog by Pat Storer
(Storey Publishing, 1997)

Useful Addresses

PDSA
Whitechapel Way
Priorslee
Telford
Shropshire
TF2 9PQ
Tel: 01952 290999
Fax: 01952 291035
Website: www.pdsa.org.uk

RSPCA
Wilberforce Way
Southwater
Horsham
West Sussex
RH13 9RS
Tel: 0870 3335 999
Fax: 0870 7530 284
Website: www.rspca.org.uk

Index